READ O

M000239642

My Sister

by Lada Josefa Kratky

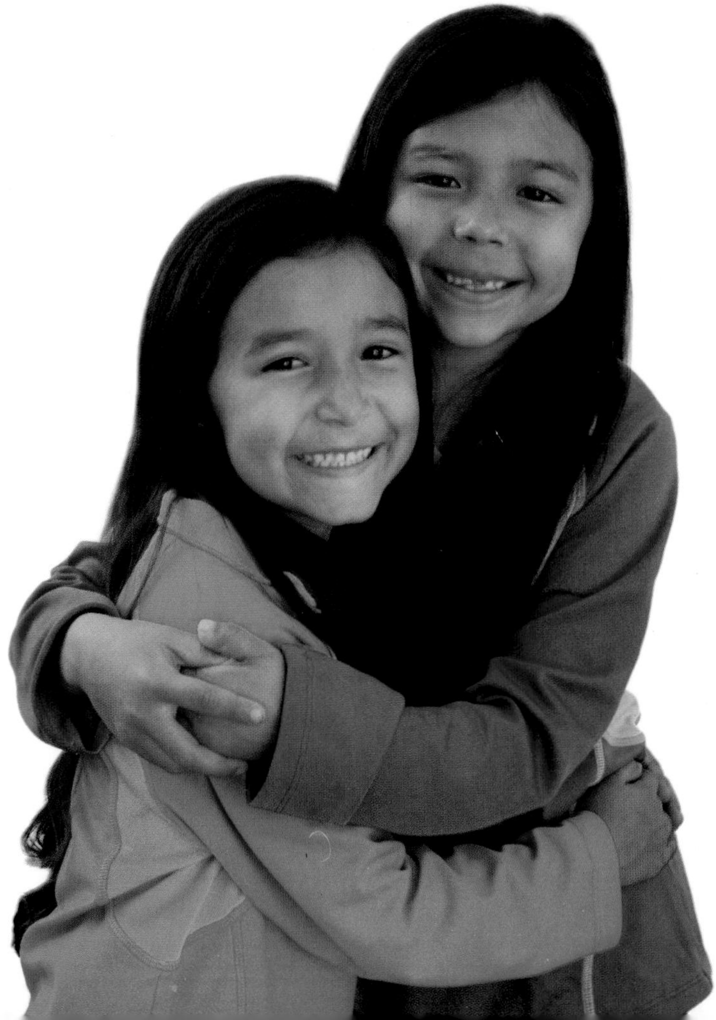

NATIONAL GEOGRAPHIC

School Publishing

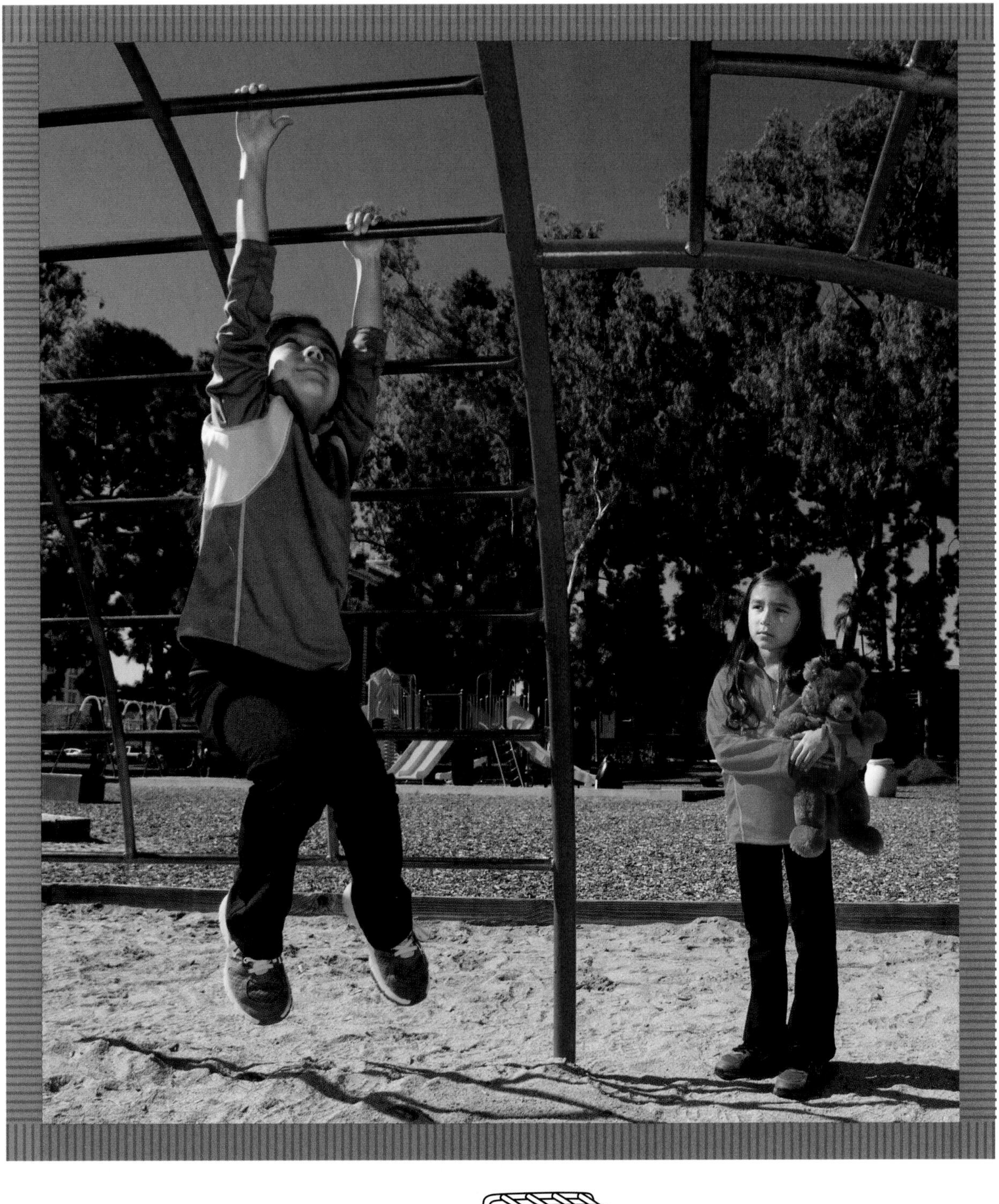

my 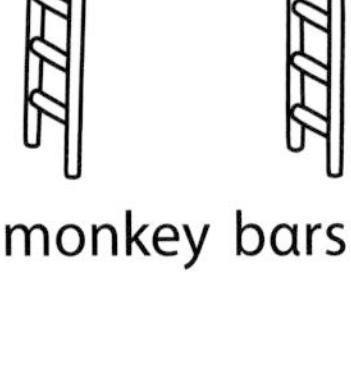

monkey bars

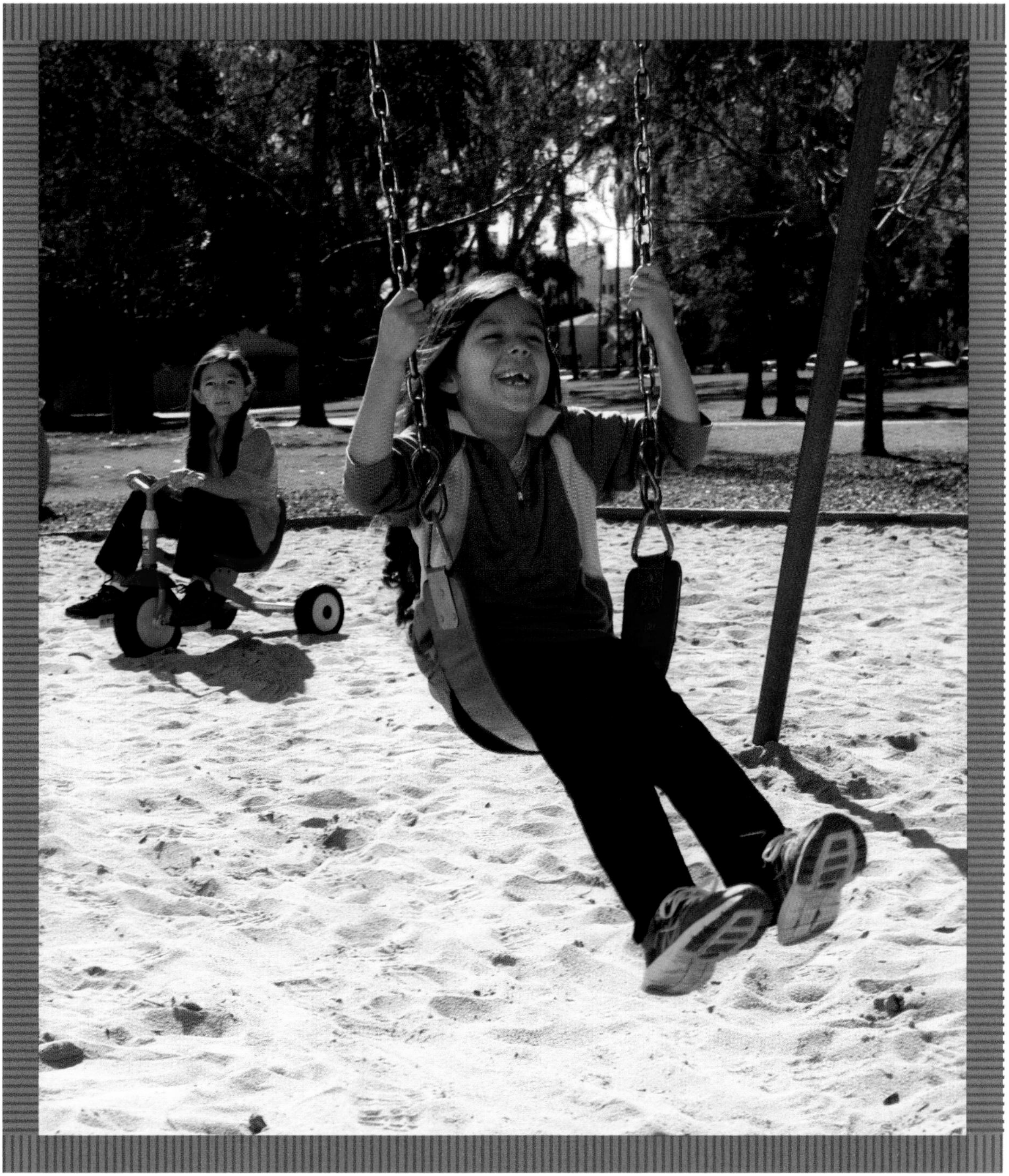

my 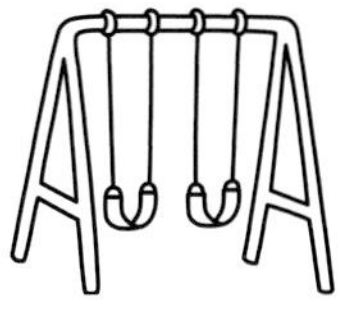 swing

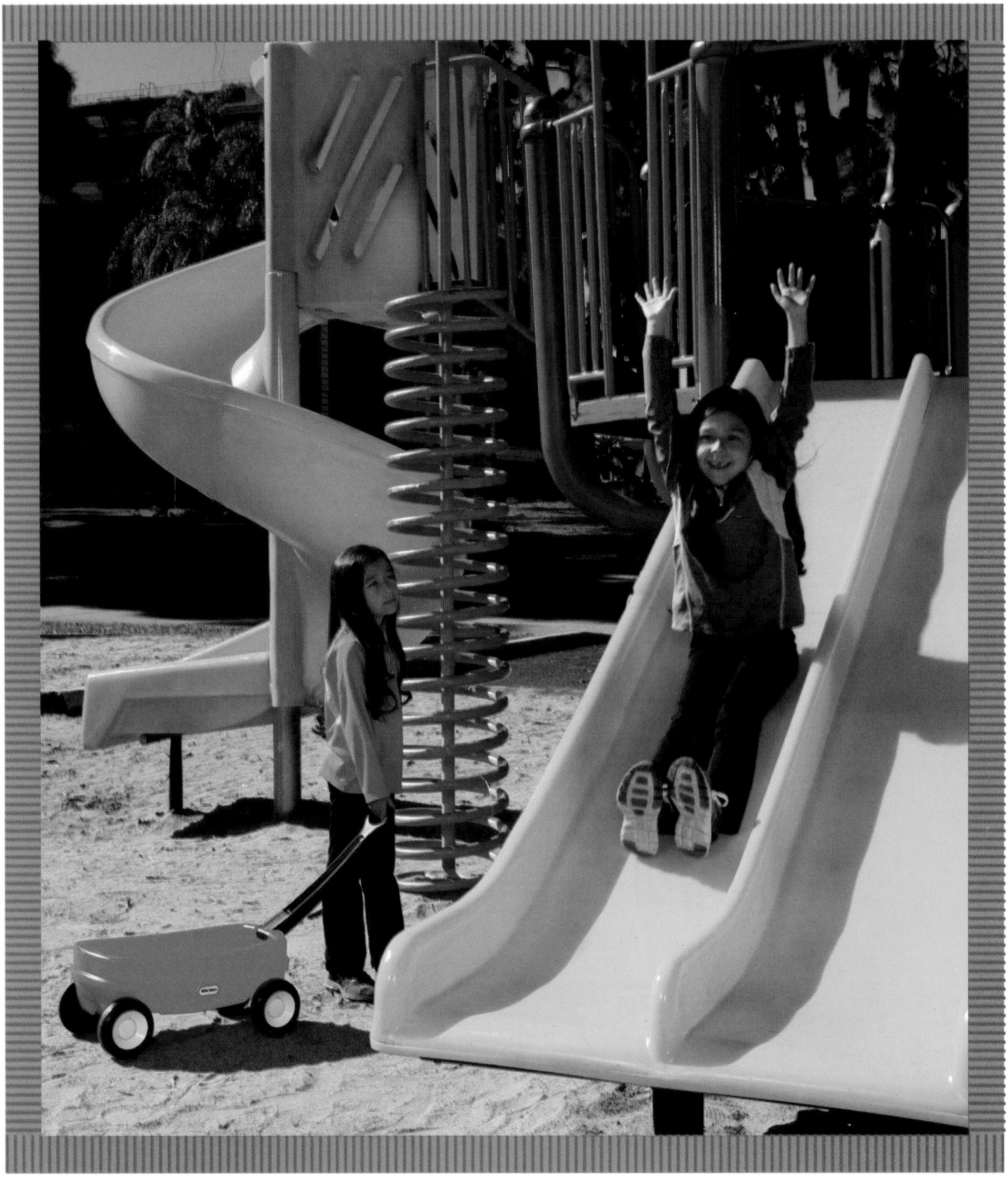

my 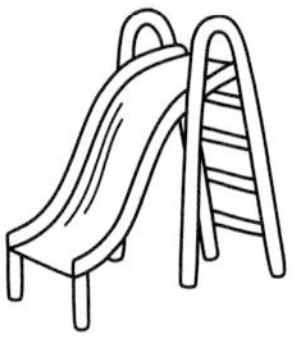
slide

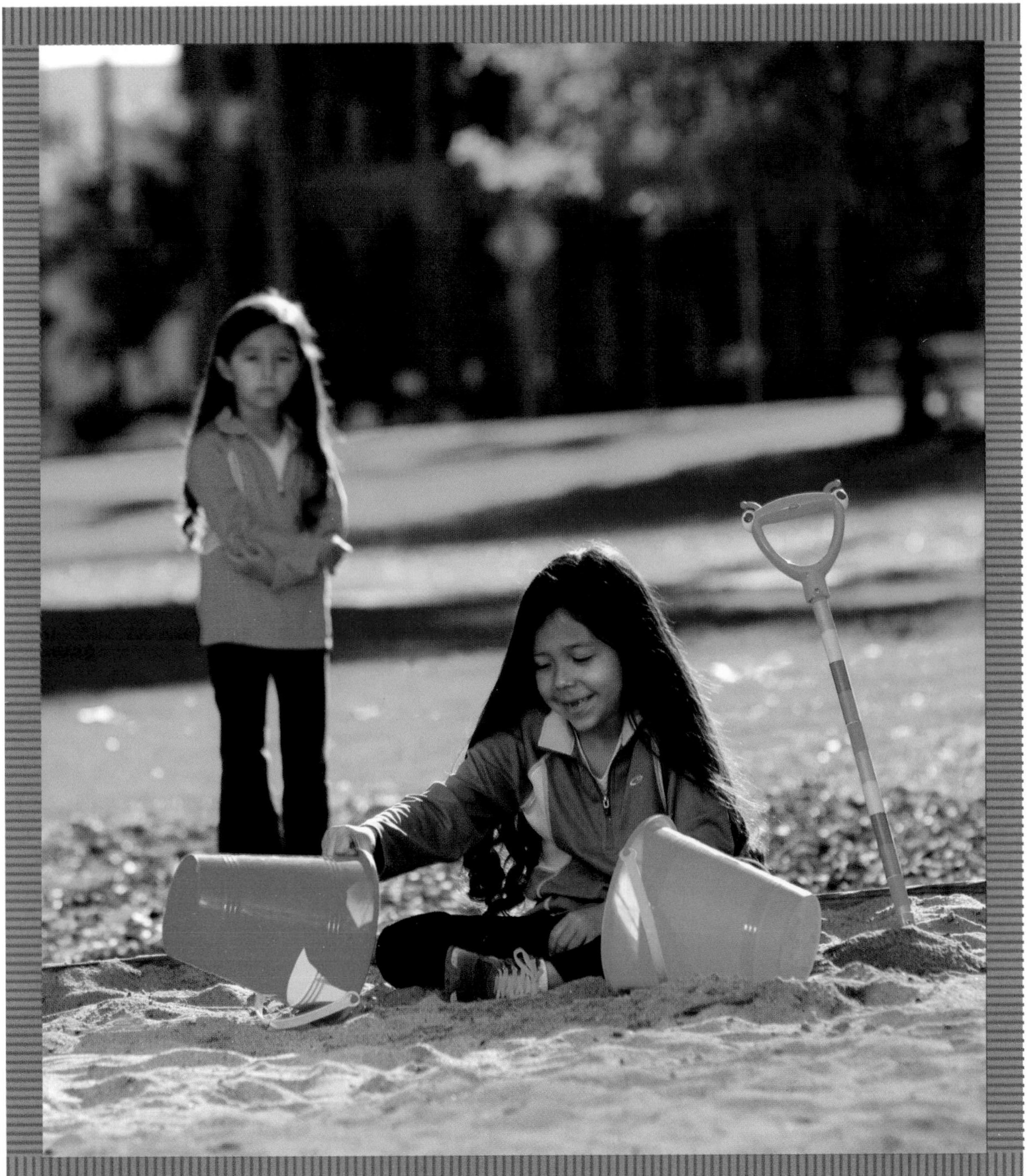

my 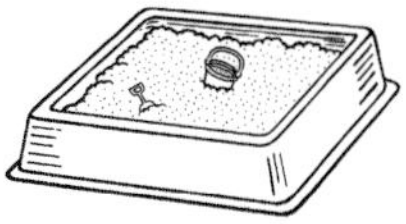

sandbox

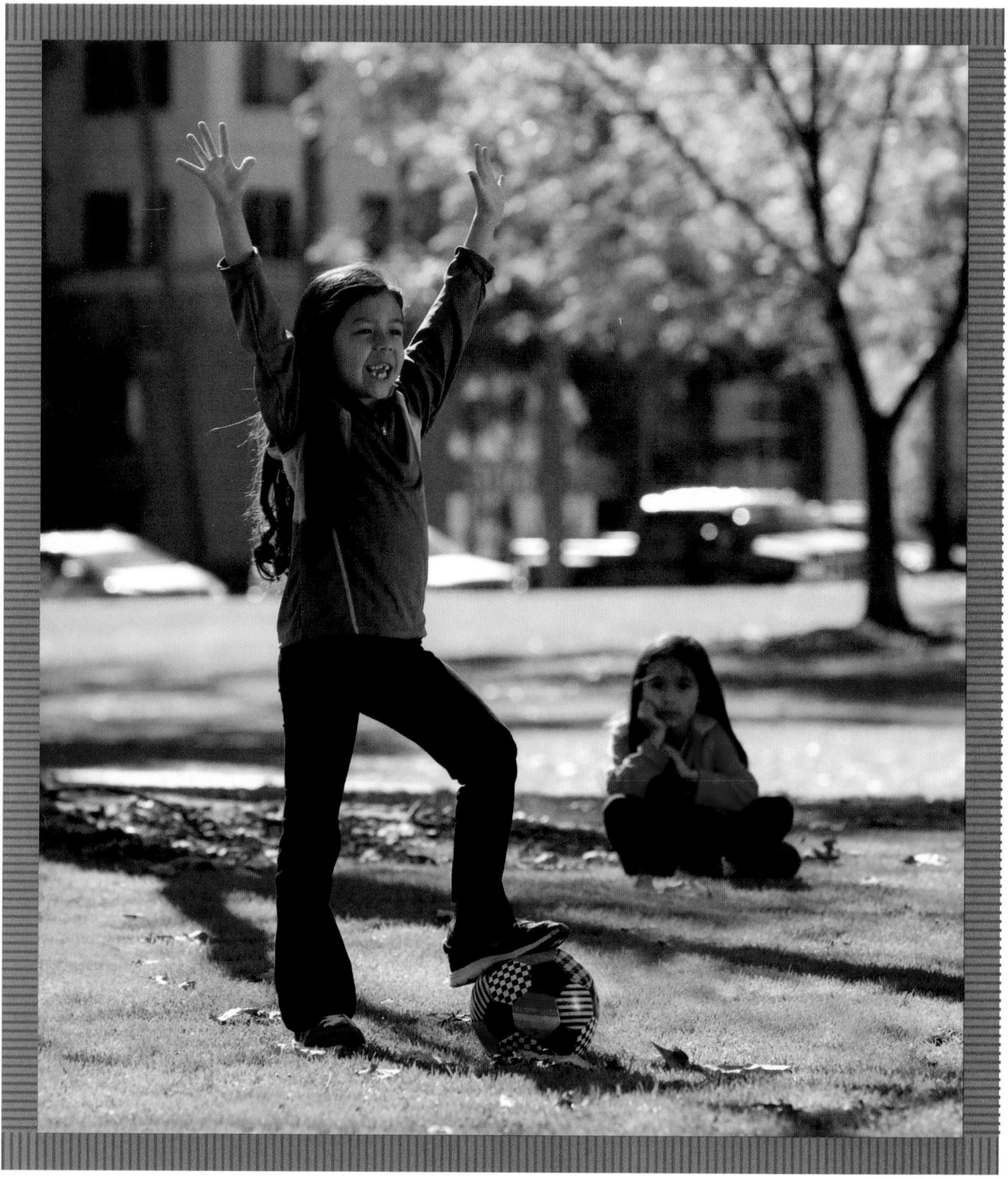

my 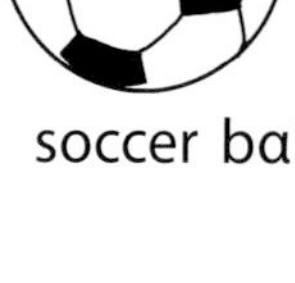

soccer ball

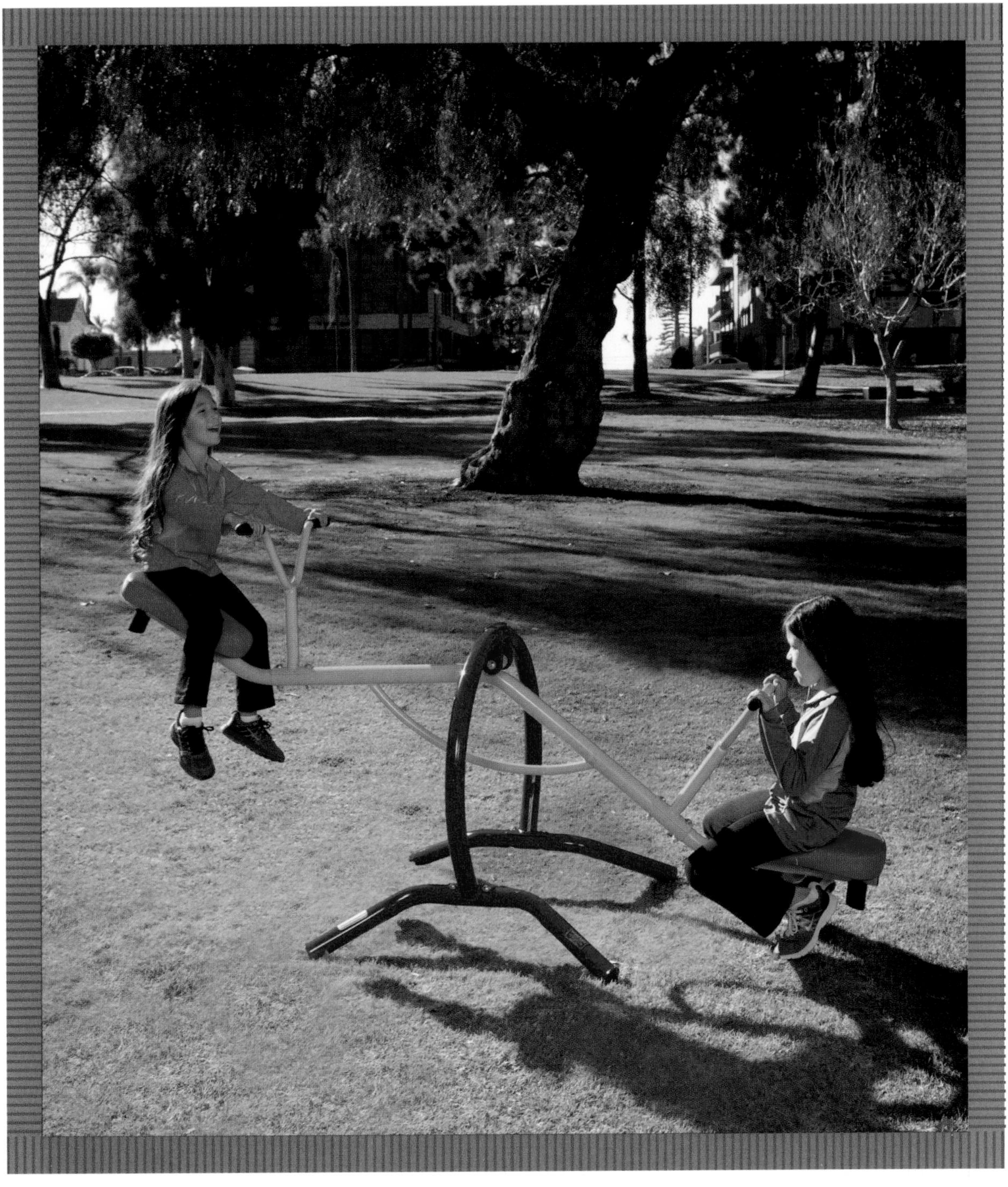

my 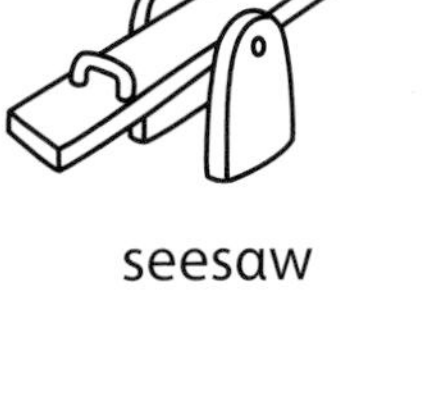

seesaw

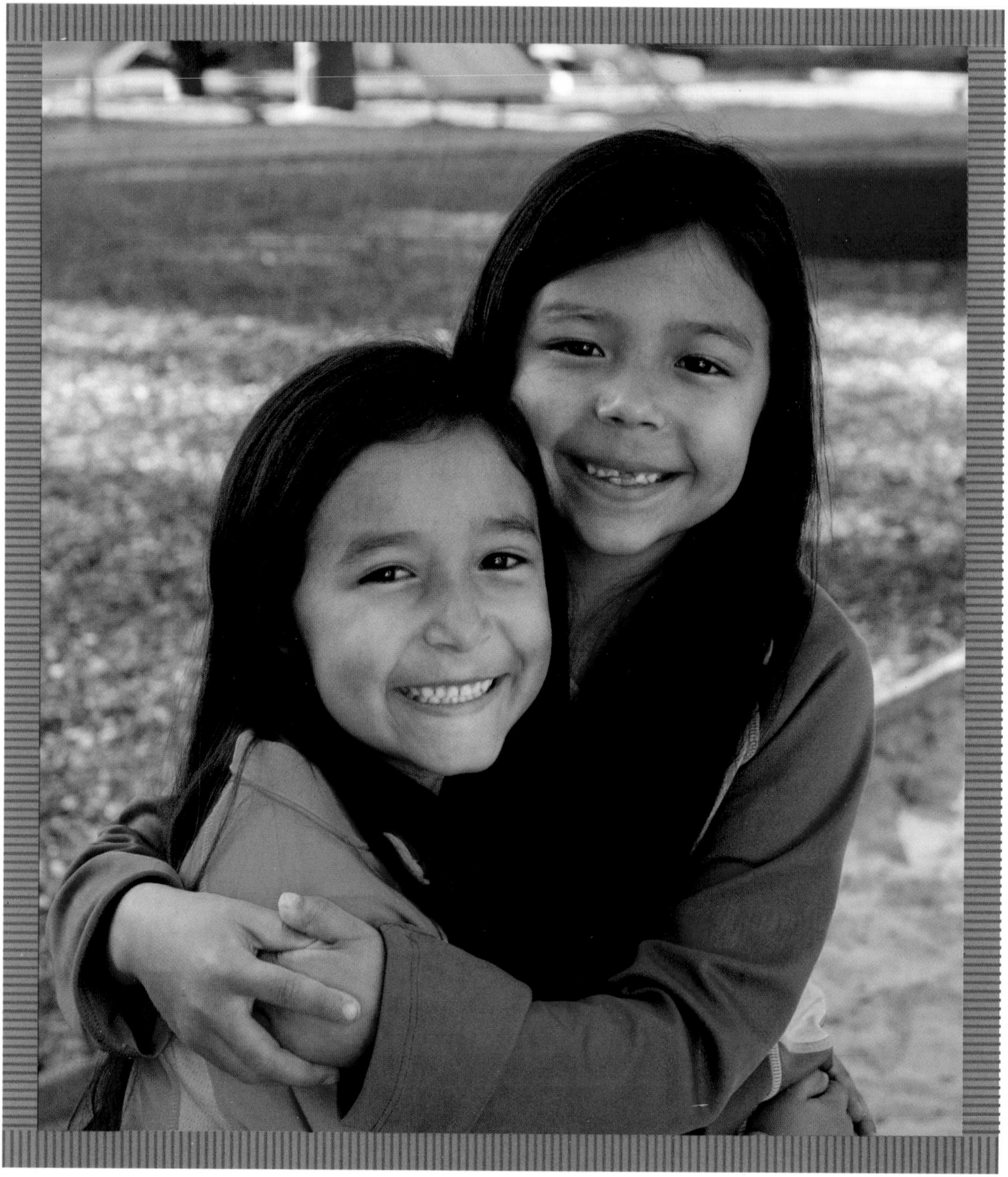

my 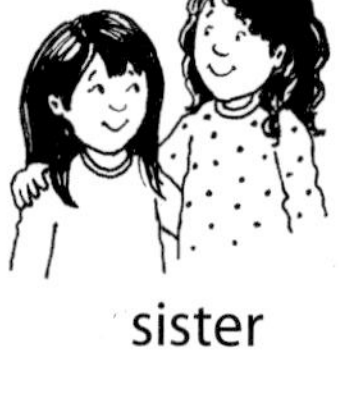

sister